Highlights
Hidden Pictures

EXTREME ADVENTURE PUZZLES

HIGHLIGHTS PRESS
Honesdale, Pennsylvania

Welcome, Hidden Pictures Puzzlers!

When you finish a puzzle, check it off √. Good luck, and happy puzzling!

Contents

Cover art by Gary LaCoste

Rain Forest Zipliners

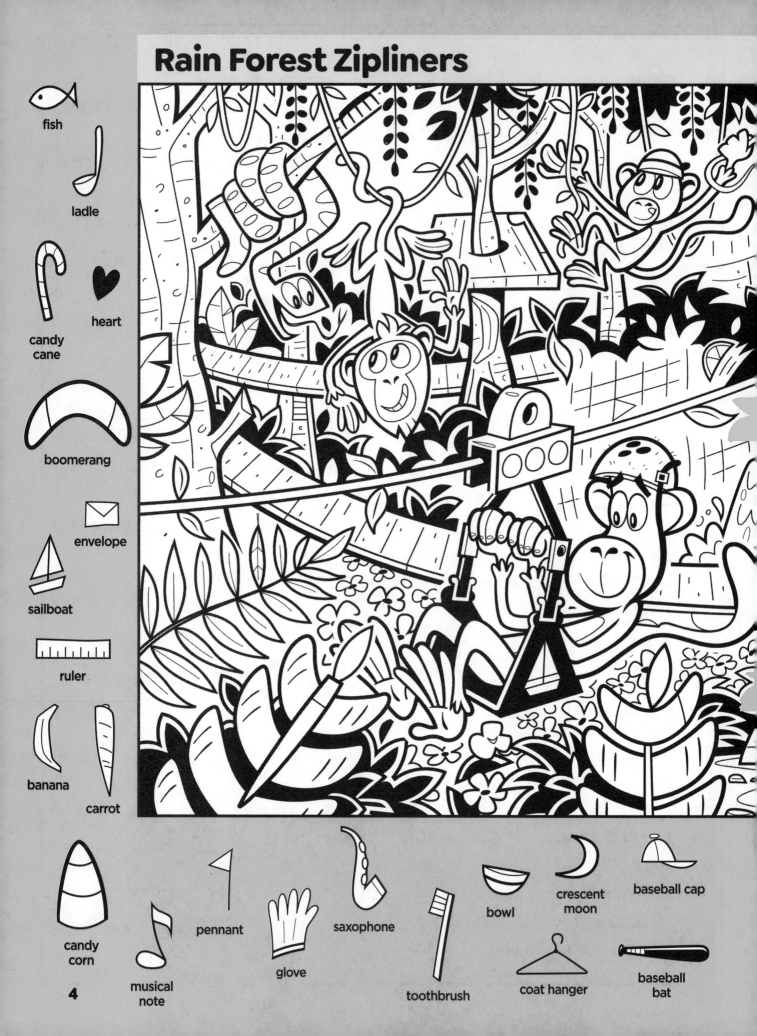

fish

ladle

candy cane

heart

boomerang

envelope

sailboat

ruler

banana

carrot

candy corn

musical note

pennant

glove

saxophone

toothbrush

bowl

crescent moon

baseball cap

coat hanger

baseball bat

golf club

tack

comb

gem

artist's brush

drinking straw

traffic light

sock

bowling pin

shoe

wedge of lemon

needle

candle

bell

slice of pizza

piece of popcorn

feather

pencil

hockey stick

Art by Gary LaCoste

5

BMX Madness

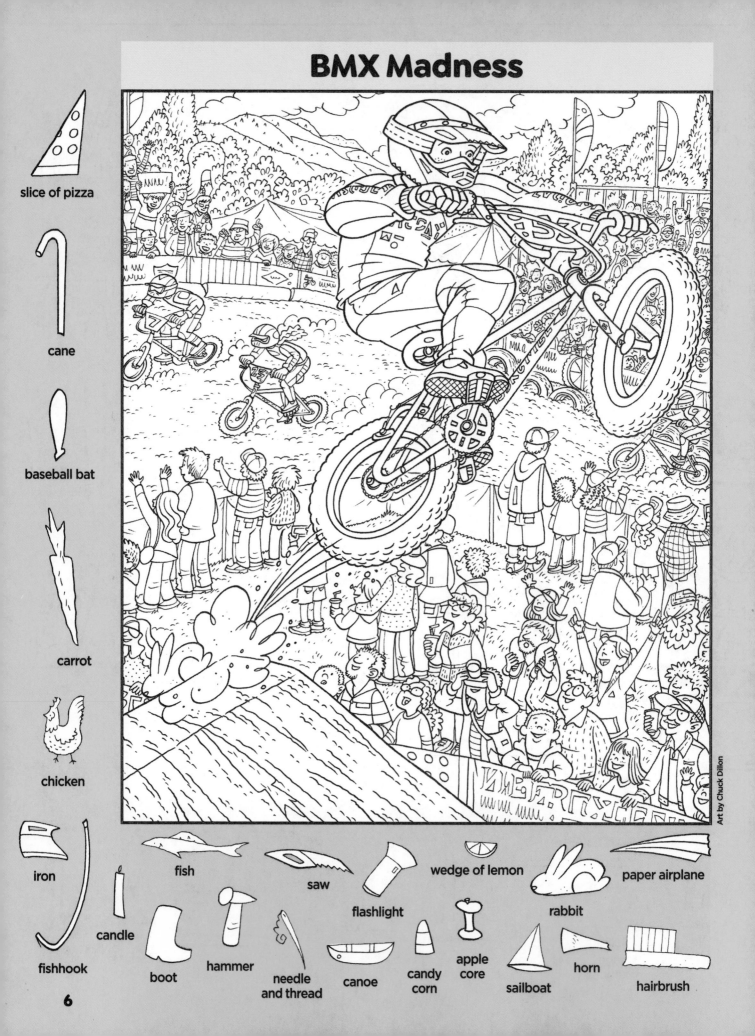

slice of pizza

cane

baseball bat

carrot

chicken

iron

fish

saw

wedge of lemon

paper airplane

flashlight

rabbit

fishhook

candle

boot

hammer

needle and thread

canoe

candy corn

apple core

sailboat

horn

hairbrush

Art by Chuck Dillon

6

Ship Ahoy!

pencil

golf club

bottle

saltshaker

ring

whistle

needle

ruler

paintbrush

spoon

leaf

cupcake

baseball cap

teacup

bell

crescent moon

Art by Mike DeSantis

Climbing Buddies

chili pepper

saltshaker

ice-cream cone

slice of bread

sailboat

bell

fish

envelope

heart

ring

wedge of cheese

open book

snail

paper airplane

cinnamon bun

piece of popcorn

slice of pizza

Art by David Bernardy

Galactic Jurassics

baseball bat

horseshoe

teacup

heart

button

envelope

butter knife

domino

saw

basketball

question mark

candle

Art by Mike Lowery

Summertime Ollies

tomato

sailboat

sock

fork

light bulb

muffin

raindrop

heart

sheep

fish

shoe

candle

needle

toothbrush

spoon

carrot

belt

oar

garden hose

10

Skydiving Skunks

fish

needle

bell

hoe

funnel

saw

book

peanut

mushroom

ring

toothbrush

envelope

football

lightning bolt

Art by Rocky Fuller

Log Flume

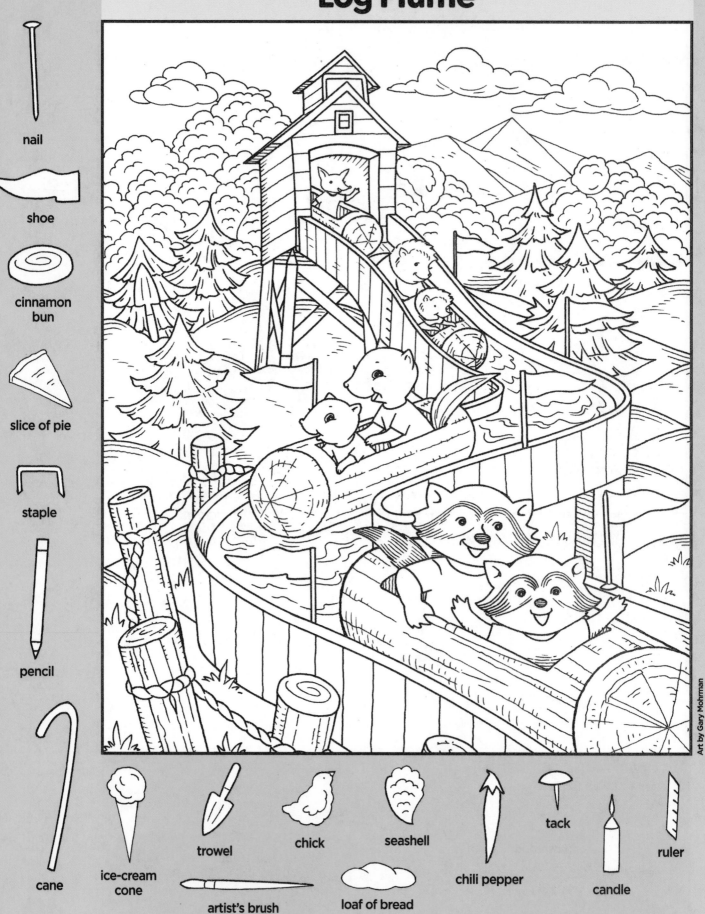

nail

shoe

cinnamon bun

slice of pie

staple

pencil

cane

ice-cream cone

trowel

artist's brush

chick

loaf of bread

seashell

chili pepper

tack

candle

ruler

Art by Gary Mohrman

12

Orb Field Day

banana

flashlight

candy corn

sailboat

ruler

wedge of cheese

baseball bat

fishing pole

slice of watermelon

ring

glove

boomerang

toaster

jump rope

slice of bread

fish

Art by Josh Cleland

13

Dino Discovery!

muffin

saltshaker

candle

apple

cherry

slice of bread

banana

teacup

musical note

nail

comb

fish

golf club

crayon

baseball bat

toothbrush

Art by Mike DeSantis

Rock-Climbing Birthday Party

bird

sock

teacup

golf club

seal

banana

spatula

heart

carrot

coffeepot

squirrel

shovel

Art by Dave Klug

And They're Off!

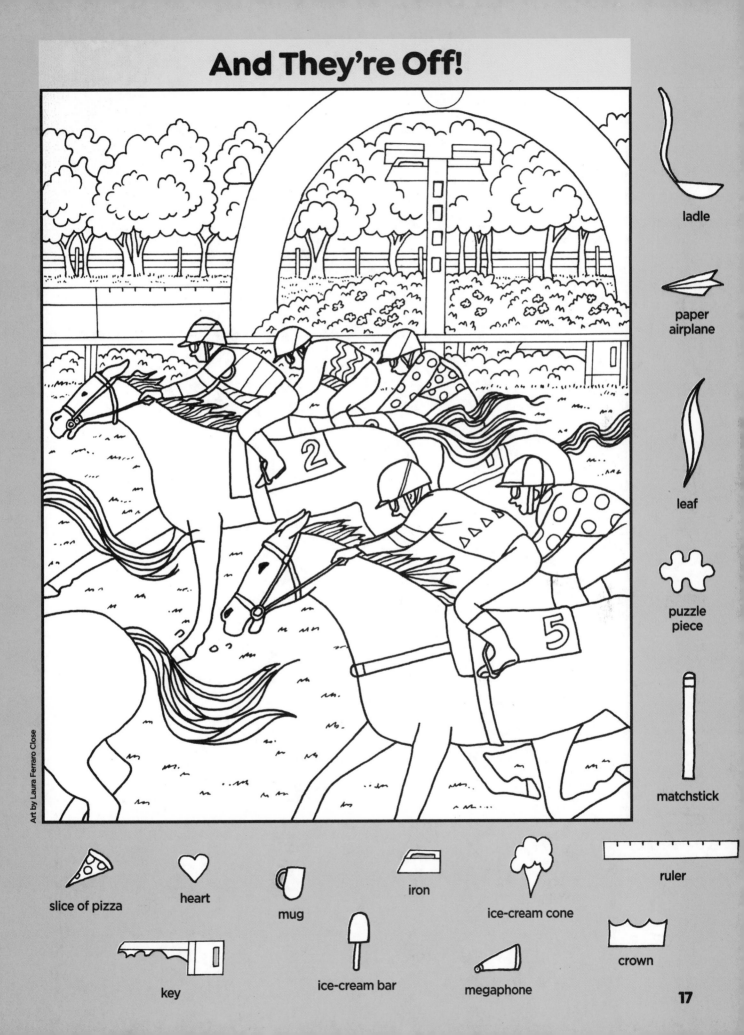

ladle

paper airplane

leaf

puzzle piece

matchstick

ruler

slice of pizza

heart

mug

iron

ice-cream cone

crown

key

ice-cream bar

megaphone

Art by Laura Ferraro Close

17

Hitting the Slopes

balloon

sailboat

needle

carrot

mushroom

piece of popcorn

heart

golf club

lollipop

teacup

bell

tack

slice of bread

envelope

candy cane

ladder

comb

ring

toothbrush

coat hanger

snow cone

snake

dinosaur

butterfly

pennant

Hang Gliding Lesson

cupcake

kite

ice-cream cone

owl

artist's brush

piece of popcorn

ice-cream bar

belt

spoon

crescent moon

ring

boomerang

golf club

paddle

hairbrush

rake

yo-yo

Art by Kelly Kennedy

19

California Sailboarding

sailboat

celery

pennant

snow cone

penguin

bird

flower

book

carrot

boot

apple

slice of pie

spoon

Art by Leslie Franz

20

Scaling the Cliffs

banana

candle

sock

golf club

crescent moon

slice of bread

frying pan

needle

pennant

fishhook

shoe

oar

fish

spoon

bell

Art by Mike DeSantis

21

Tropical Tour

crown

heart

ice-cream bar

drinking straw

needle

piece of popcorn

coat hanger

sock

ruler

balloon

lima bean

artist's brush

waffle

carrot

toothbrush

candle

hammer

canoe

22

glove

spoon

bowl

hockey stick

bell   fishhook

pennant

pine tree

comb

crescent moon

wedge of lemon

magnet

mitten

banana

drumstick

ladle

envelope

scissors

golf club

Art by Gary LaCoste

23

Bounce House Bonanza

mushroom

candle

drinking straw

nail

toothbrush

Art by David Bernardy

pennant

paper airplane

bird

canoe

muffin

shoe

slice of pizza

sailboat

slice of pie

24

Serious Air

needle

heart

artist's brush

banana

arrow

drinking glass

toothbrush

mallet

Art by Mary Sullivan

Keeping Track

teacup

hairbrush

french fries

pie

bird

shark

flashlight

glove

mop

heart

wristwatch

mushroom

closed umbrella

fish

Art by Jacob Chabot

In the Wheelhouse

2 drumsticks

croquet mallet

lightning bolt

eyeglasses

light bulb

scarf

wedge of lemon

crescent moon

egg

potato

muffin

chick

arrow

exclamation point

pear

Art by Scot Ritchie

Snowboard Style

mushroom

screwdriver

arrow

golf club

spatula

worm

flag

crescent
moon

heart

scissors

egg

teacup

banana

sponge

iron

Art by Rocky Fuller

29

Gymnastics Practice

mallet

glove

teapot

dessert dish

pencil

musical note

mug

crown

shoe

seashell

hand mirror

coat hanger

wrench

bell

arrow

golf club

eyeglasses

30

Riding the Rapids

slice of pie

pencil

spoon

teacup

slice of pizza

banana

carrot

handbell

heart

turtle

glove

toothbrush

Art by Tim Davis

31

Surface Skimmers

ruler

gingerbread cookie

bottle

heart

artist's brush

teacup

glove

slice of bread

nail

open book

sock

pencil

saw

megaphone

Art by Tim Davis

Tomb Explorers

golf club

boomerang

snow cone

whistle

chili pepper

fish

carrot

fried egg

pennant

olive

mushroom

bird

slice of pizza

sailboat

envelope

musical note

eyeglasses

pencil

cupcake

T-shirt

tomato

Art by Bill Golliher

33

High, Higher, Highest

ruler

apple

crayon

saltshaker

baseball cap

book

duck

candle

crown

umbrella

pennant

shoe

Art by Mike DeSantis

35

Bungee Trampolines

nail

envelope

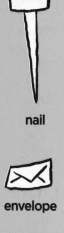
ladder

olive

ruler

crescent moon

teacup

domino

snake

needle

party hat

bell

elbow noodle

mitten

pencil

peanut

toy top

Art by Brian Michael Weaver

36

Tubing Slope

book

shoe

crescent moon

chili pepper

heart

funnel

candle

pepper

wishbone

sailboat

canoe

butter knife

nail

envelope

seashell

boomerang

arrow

slice of pizza

Art by Gary Mohrman

Sunken Treasure

iron

envelope

artist's brush

trowel

comb

cake

fried egg

muffin

Art by Patrick Girouard

38

Up and Away!

crescent moon

glove

banana

candy cane

magnet

computer

needle

musical note

can opener

pencil

sailboat

spool of thread

spoon

football

Art by Rocky Fuller

Barrel Rolls

handbell

heart

caterpillar

slice of pizza

open book

teacup

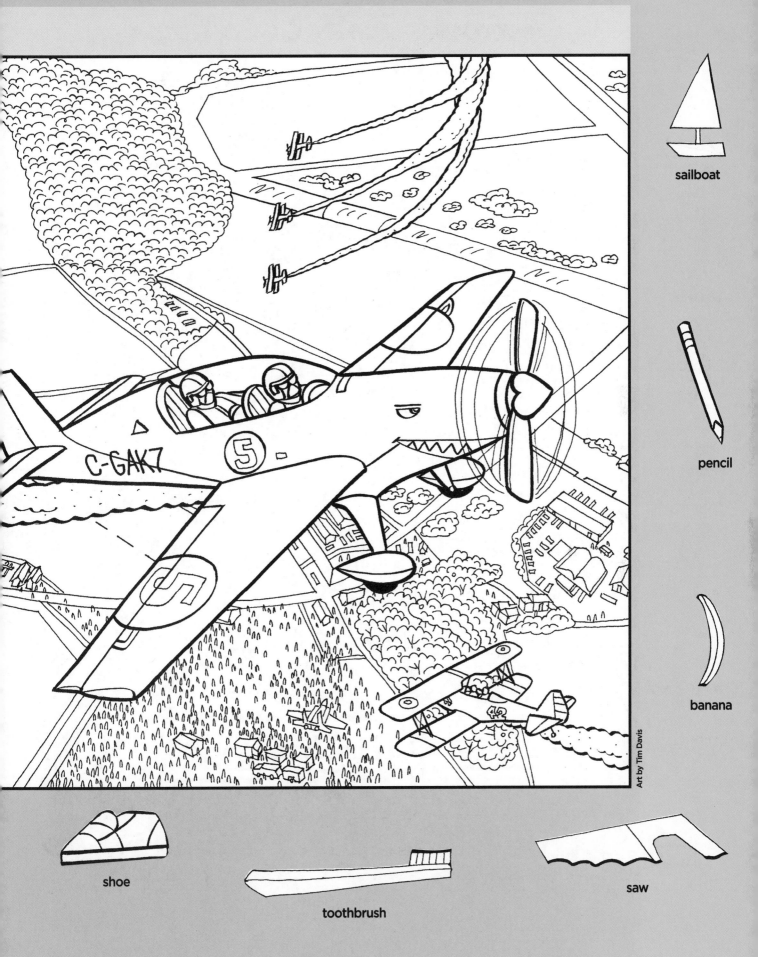

sailboat

pencil

banana

shoe

toothbrush

saw

Art by Tim Davis

41

Astronomically Good Pizza

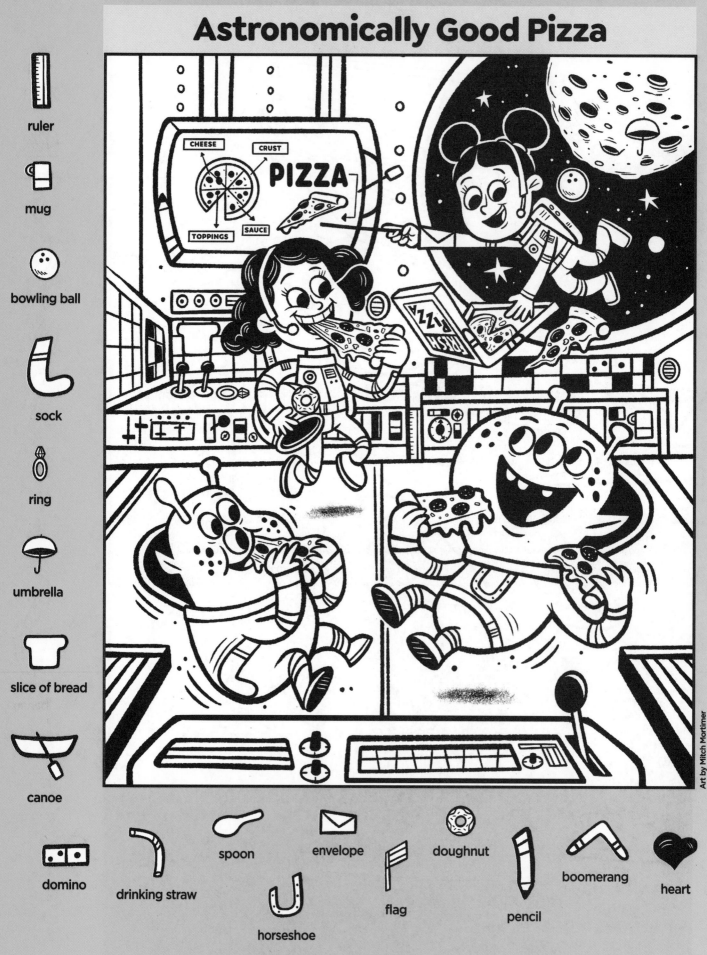

ruler

mug

bowling ball

sock

ring

umbrella

slice of bread

canoe

domino

drinking straw

spoon

envelope

doughnut

pencil

boomerang

heart

flag

horseshoe

Art by Mitch Mortimer

Owls on Ice

artist's brush

banana

wishbone

trowel

pennant

bell

teacup

boomerang

shoe

leaf

gravy boat

chili pepper

frying pan

envelope

candle

heart

canoe

building block

Art by Gary Mohrman

43

Splashy Serve

flashlight

ladle

hockey stick

pickax

sailboat

knitted hat

adhesive bandage

dog bone

pencil

ladder

bat

scissors

domino

Art by Jacob Chabot

The Great Question

banana

heart

tack

paper clip

bell

sailboat

needle

slice of pie

toothbrush

fish

megaphone

pencil

glove

eyeglasses

46

Go-Kart Giraffes

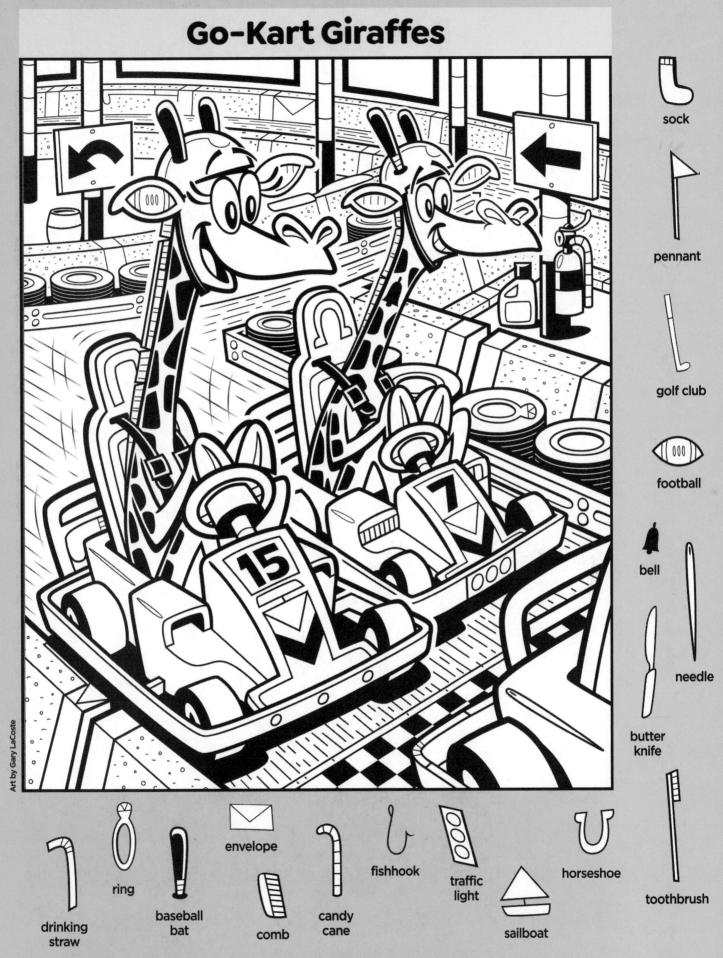

sock

pennant

golf club

football

bell

needle

butter knife

toothbrush

drinking straw

ring

baseball bat

envelope

comb

candy cane

fishhook

traffic light

sailboat

horseshoe

Art by Gary LaCoste

Everybody Hoops!

heart

lollipop

eyeglasses

mushroom

banana

toothbrush

waffle

fishhook

Art by Pat Lewis

pennant

ring

pencil

boomerang

slice of pie

glove

teacup

cane

carrot

domino

pine tree

scooter

All-Terrain Pals

candle

butter knife

candy cane

bean

sailboat

duck

ice-cream cone

paper clip

pencil

peanut

knitted hat

paper airplane

spoon

bowl

shoe

slice of pizza

bell

Art by Mary Sullivan

One Wild Contest

heart

balloon

baseball cap

needle

artist's brush

hockey stick

pencil

ice-cream bar

sneaker

mug

ladder

drinking straw

snake

top hat

ring

crown

boomerang

coat hanger

feather

crescent moon

envelope

fishhook

pennant

bowl

toothbrush

ice-cream cone

wedge of lemon

paper clip

horseshoe

Art by Gary LaCoste

yardstick

sock

piece of popcorn

bell

candle

traffic light

baseball

tack

banana

pair of pants

51

Crabbing on the Bay

toothbrush

closed umbrella

golf club

heart

party hat

open book

bowl

artist's brush

shoe

crescent moon

pen

glove

paddle

mushroom

ice-cream cone

fork

Art by Chuck Dillon

52

Spelunking

snake

adhesive bandage

glove

button

crescent moon

carrot

tack

sock

bowling pin

ice-cream bar

teacup

ruler

artist's brush

comb

ice-cream cone

envelope

yo-yo

pencil

potato

slice of pizza

frying pan

Art by Brian Michael Weaver

A Snowy Trek

banana

popcorn

butterfly

crown

clothespin

fishhook

jellyfish

sock

jump rope

paper airplane

sailboat

boomerang

pencil

needle

toothbrush

wedge of lemon

wishbone

yo-yo

coat hanger

fish

necktie

open book

muffin

heart

fork

fried egg

candy corn

spool of thread

teacup

tack

Art by Laura Ferraro Close

Rail Biking

fish

book

mug

flyswatter

cupcake

pencil

needle

ice-cream
bar

glove

bowling
pin

wedge of
orange

arrow

bat

funnel

fork

magnet

slice of
cake

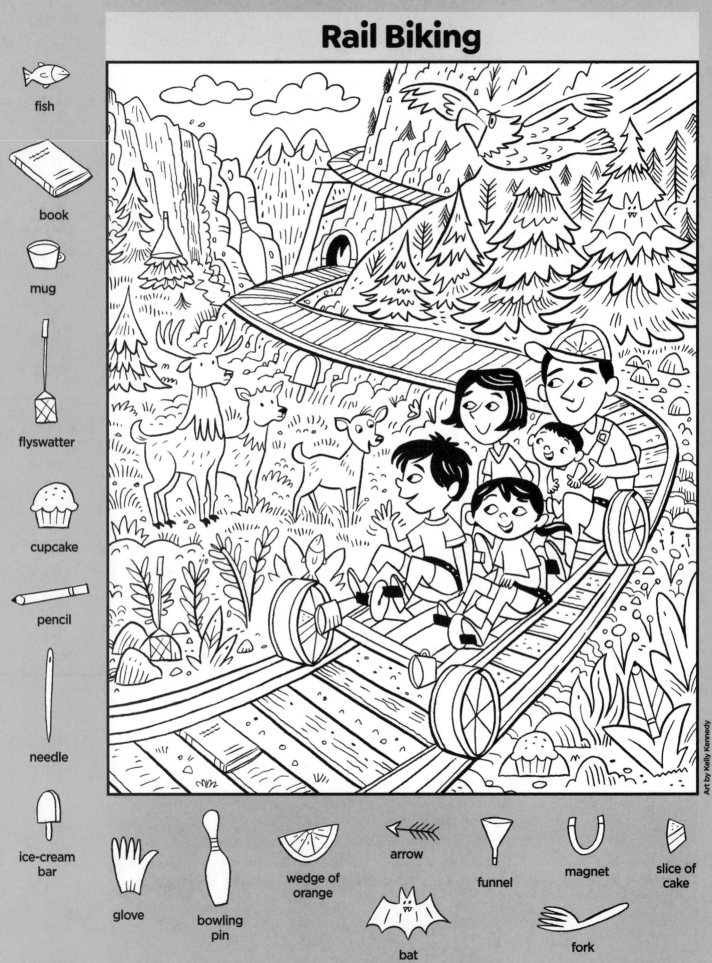

Art by Kelly Kennedy

56

Fun in the Waves

hammer

apple

needle

nail

mushroom

pair of shorts

crescent moon

banana

sock

carrot

heart

pencil

ladle

toothbrush

mitten

Art by R. Michael Palan

Biking the Trail

toothbrush

whistle

artist's brush

mushroom

mitten

drinking cup

gem

flashlight

lollipop

heart

snake

pencil

hockey stick

chili pepper

closed umbrella

slice of pizza

bowl

carrot

Art by Jennifer Harney

Picture Day

waffle

knitted hat

teacup

slice of pizza

comb

ice-cream bar

crescent moon

crayon

slice of cheese

drinking straw

boot

olive

heart

flag

wishbone

boomerang

fried egg

eyeglasses

Art by Pat Lewis

59

Wild Paddlers

glove

fork

mitten

banana

handbell

saw

sock

pencil

leaf

crescent
moon

nail

ladle

Art by Iryna Bodnaruk

Zipping Along

lollipop

glove

paper clip

flag

slice of pie

artist's brush

pennant

heart

eyeglasses

crescent moon

knitted hat

open book

yo-yo

fried egg

envelope

needle

flashlight

Art by Deborah Johnson

Our First Hike

fish

candy corn

teacup

stapler

pennant

arrow

fishhook

needle

jump rope

worm

belt

banana

coat hanger

wedge of lemon

hard hat

heart

potato

book

Art by Scot Ritchie

Dino Divers

ring

light bulb

lollipop

hot dog

closed umbrella

glove

crescent moon

eyeglasses

adhesive bandage

comb

balloon

baseball

Art by Mike Lowery

The Heist

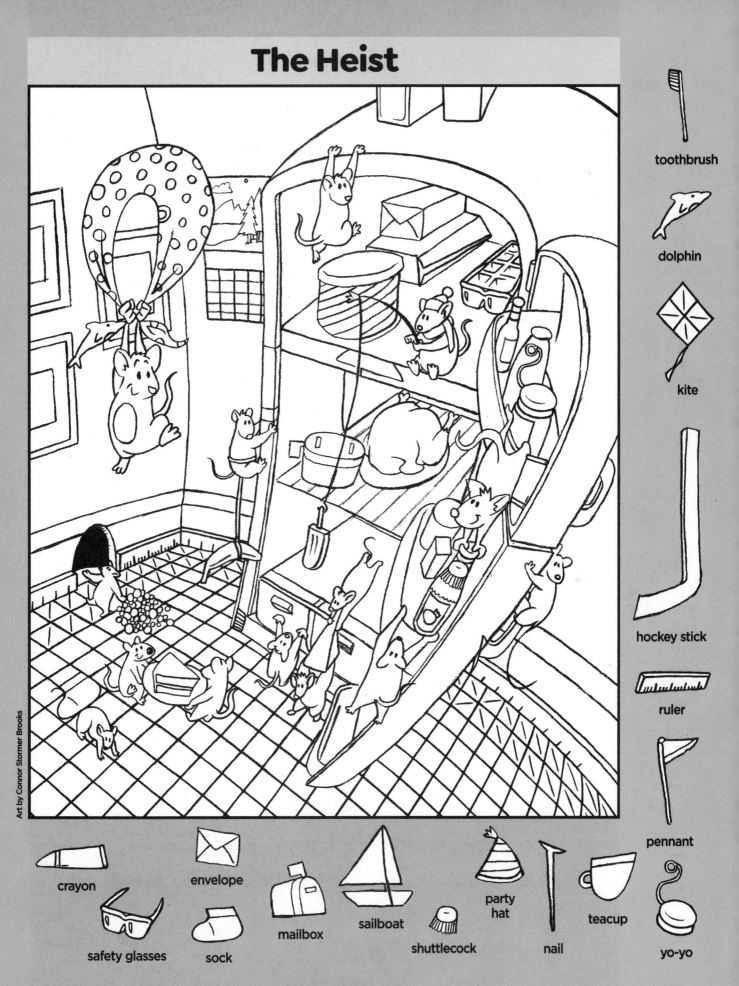

toothbrush

dolphin

kite

hockey stick

ruler

pennant

crayon

envelope

mailbox

sailboat

party hat

teacup

yo-yo

safety glasses

sock

shuttlecock

nail

Art by Connor Stormer Brooks

65

Panda on a Half Pipe

heart

toothbrush

drinking straw

canoe

crescent moon

sailboat

bowl

traffic light

ruler

mushroom

snow cone

wedge of orange

tack

coat hanger

envelope

banana

needle

bell

lollipop

flag

horseshoe

hockey stick

Art by Gary LaCoste

66

Ropes Course

Art by Pat Lewis

Can you find 12 pencils hidden in this scene?

Dreaming of Adventure

snowman

chili pepper

frying pan

green bean

pointy hat

envelope

crescent moon

artist's palette

propeller hat

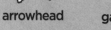
arrowhead

game piece

flashlight

golf club

nail

worm

olive

Canoe Trip

slice of bread

trowel

spoon

light bulb

gem

whistle

shrimp

seashell

carrot

ice-cream bar

fork

mushroom

wishbone

artist's brush

toothbrush

pencil

Art by Leighanne Schneider

Swing Time

fish

airplane

fork

leaf

lollipop

feather

kite

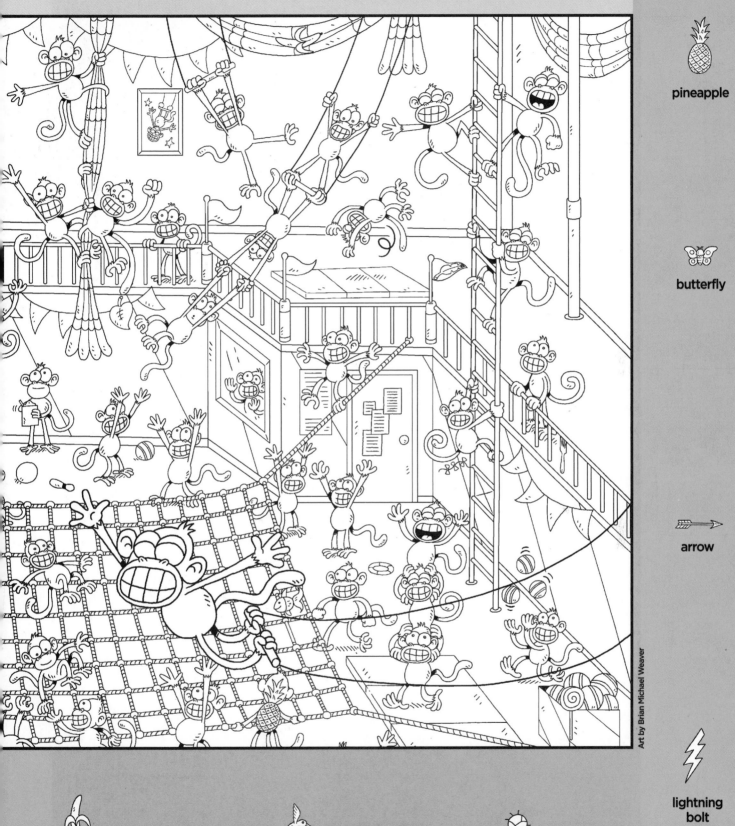

pineapple

butterfly

arrow

lightning
bolt

banana

hummingbird

ladybug

Art by Brian Michael Weaver

71

Cliffside Critters

crown

flashlight

broccoli

tack

carrot

comb

drumstick

lightning bolt

mitten

slice of pie

canoe

hockey stick

toothbrush

artist's brush

bowl

ladle

spatula

Art by Brian Michael Weaver

72

Rowdy Rollers

musical note

sock

mushroom

lightning bolt

feather

heart

traffic cone

saucepan

magnet

top hat

boomerang

canoe

sailboat

arrow

crown

Art by Sonya Montenegro

Exploring the Lake

chili pepper

tooth

fried egg

musical note

spoon

crown

flag

closed umbrella

banana

nail

belt

candy cane

key

flashlight

ice-cream cone

Art by Scot Ritchie

74

Professional Bull Rider

cotton candy

ice-cream bar

hot dog

party hat

giraffe

egret

heart

flashlight

seal

golf club

tree

paintbrush

boomerang

ax

closed umbrella

pennant

fish

fire extinguisher

Art by Chuck Dillon

Road Runner Race

arrow

slice of watermelon

open book

needle

cane

pointy hat

fried egg

matchstick

paper clip

mitten

golf club

ruler

magic wand

76

star

wishbone

button

slice of pie

fish

lightning bolt

spatula

heart

horn

sock

artist's brush

piece of popcorn

Art by Laura Ferarro Close

77

Salmon Run Fun

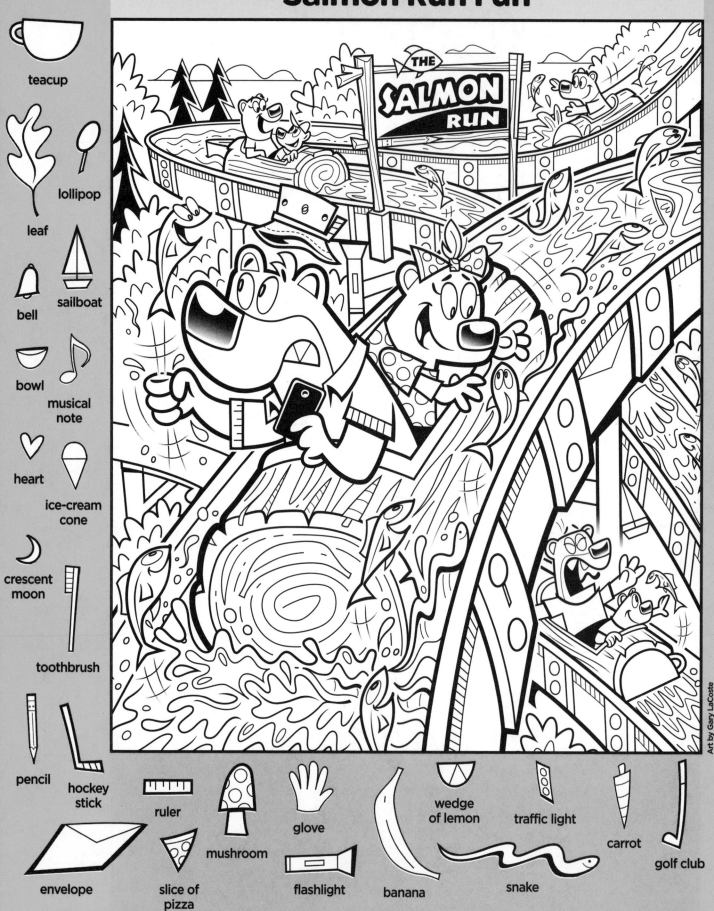

teacup

lollipop

leaf

sailboat

bell

bowl

musical note

heart

ice-cream cone

crescent moon

toothbrush

pencil

hockey stick

ruler

mushroom

glove

wedge of lemon

traffic light

carrot

golf club

envelope

slice of pizza

flashlight

banana

snake

Art by Gary LaCoste

Obstacle Course Finals

bowl

bowling ball

pickax

carrot

feather

needle

golf club

shovel

drinking straw

candle

sock

spoon

cell phone

orange

canoe

sailboat

flashlight

ruler

crown

ring

teacup

toothbrush

Art by Brian Michael Weaver

Balloon Tour

bell

lollipop

megaphone

spoon

seal

light bulb

whisk broom

rolling pin

fish

tea bag

funnel

heart

bowl

open book

Art by George Wildman

80

Race Day

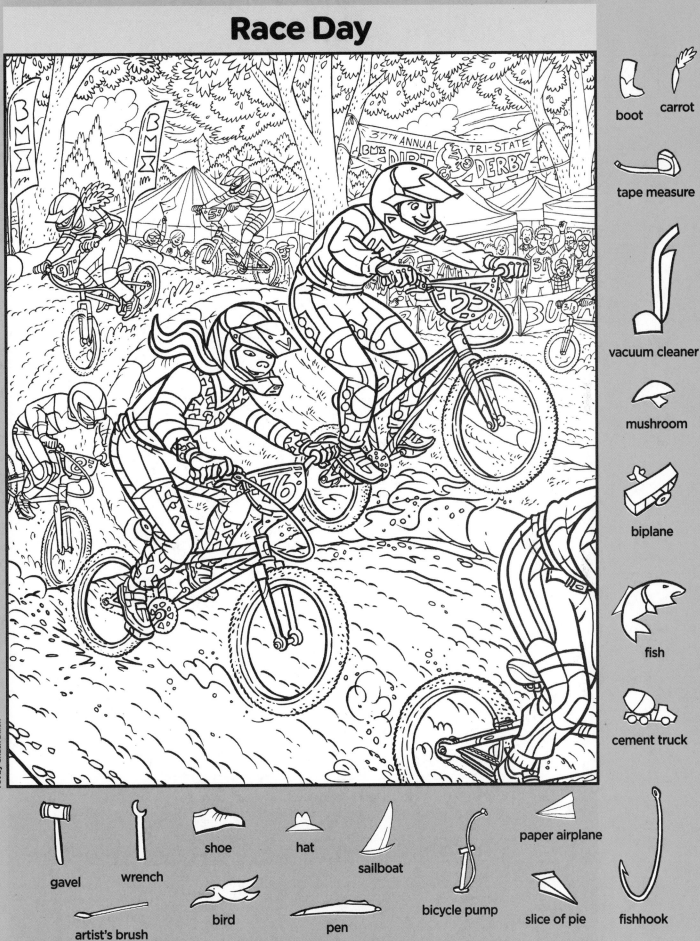

boot
carrot
tape measure
vacuum cleaner
mushroom
biplane
fish
cement truck

gavel
wrench
shoe
hat
sailboat
paper airplane
artist's brush
bird
pen
bicycle pump
slice of pie
fishhook

Art by Chuck Dillon

A Whale of a Time

candle

ice-cream cone

ruler

toothbrush

crescent moon

nail

pencil

baseball cap

golf club

needle

banana

pumpkin

can

sunglasses

mug

heart

Art by Mike DeSantis

83

Mole Patrol

bird

seashell

boomerang

snake

heart

feather

flag

crescent moon

elf's hat

ice-cream cone

shoe

fish

baseball bat

vase

boot

banana

sock

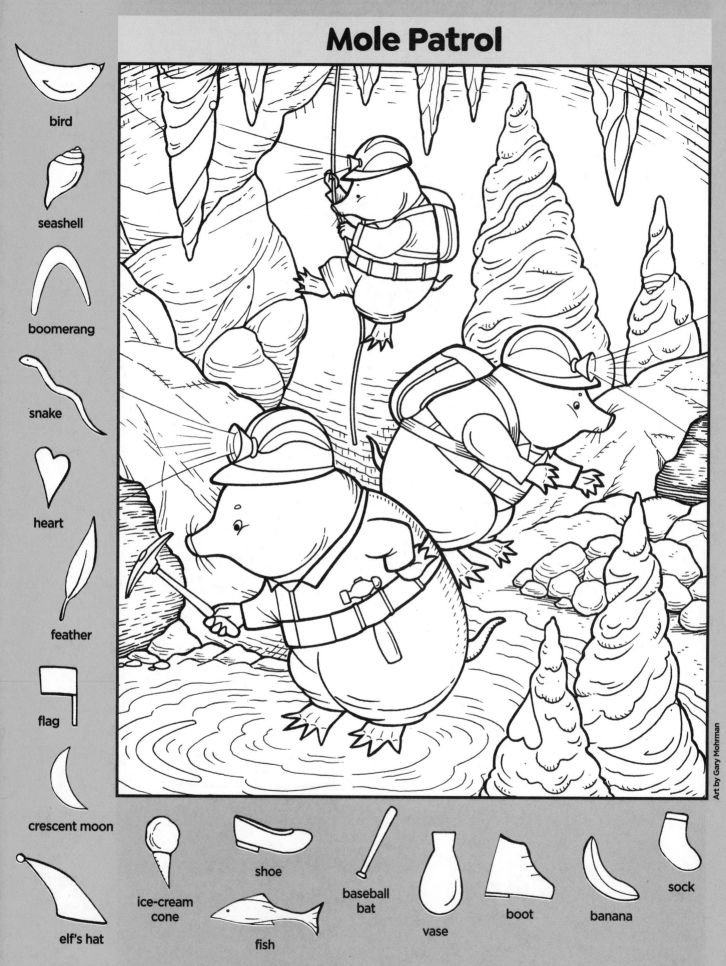

Art by Gary Mohrman

84

Wild Bumper Cars

golf club

boot

lollipop

bell

leaf

crown

slice of bread

toothbrush

pencil

crescent moon

envelope

teacup

sock

top hat

slice of watermelon

pair of shorts

Art by R. Michael Palan

Log Rolling

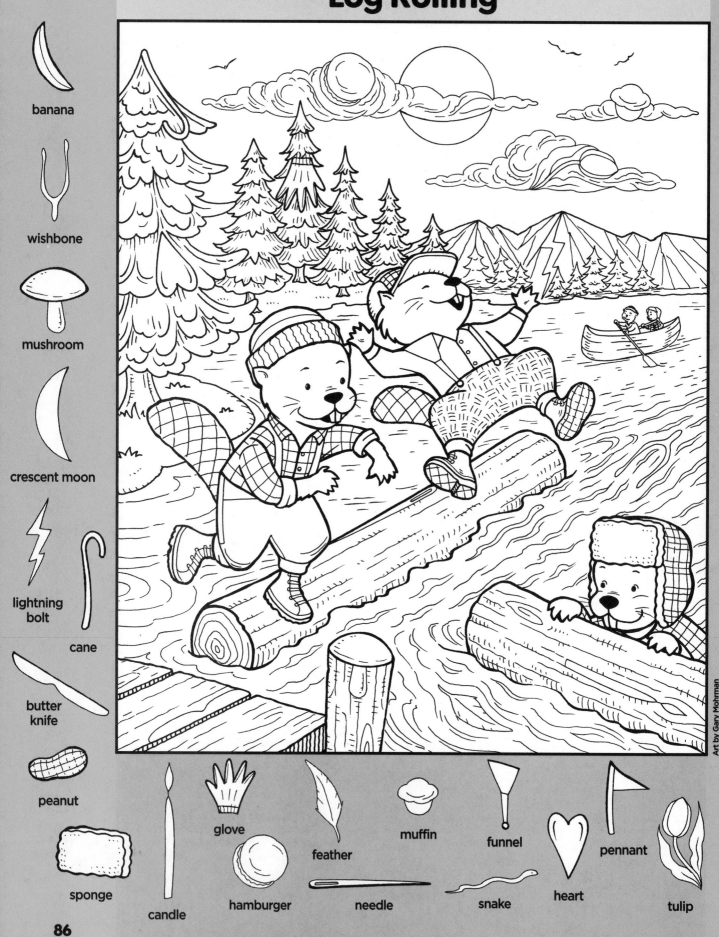

banana

wishbone

mushroom

crescent moon

lightning bolt

cane

butter knife

peanut

sponge

candle

glove

hamburger

feather

needle

muffin

funnel

snake

heart

pennant

tulip

Art by Gary Mohrman

86

Snowboarding at Heart

golf tee

yo-yo

green bean

star

lollipop

candle

muffin

hammer

teardrop

teacup

sheep

snake

slice of pie

button

sock

candy corn

arrow

fish

crown

ice-cream cone

eyeglasses

cane

Art by Laura Ferraro Close

87

The Party Trail

artist's brush

candle

muffin

flag

key

pencil

teacup

88

pitcher

musical note

fork

glove

hat

wishbone

crescent moon

comb

crown

Art by Mike DeSantis

Otter Slip and Slide

umbrella

bat

artist's brush

fork

boot

horseshoe

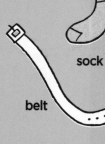
belt

sock

pitcher

pencil

spoon

scissors

glove

crown

teacup

eyeglasses

yo-yo

slice of bread

Art by Kelly Kennedy

Dormant Volcano Tour

beet

cupcake

crescent moon

teacup

ruler

frog

envelope

bird

crown

banana

toothbrush

snake

sailboat

slice of pizza

fish

Art by Tamara Petrosino

Lunar Trampoline Park

baseball bat

teacup

bell

bowling ball

comb

three-leaf clover

sailboat

ruler

crown

waffle

boomerang

ring

iron

envelope

pencil

golf club

dumbbell

flashlight

sock

spatula

Diving Pool

eyeglasses

crown

fishhook

necktie

candle

boomerang

pointy hat

snail

comb

crescent moon

egg

clover

snake

star

banana

diamond

slice of pie

Art by Gary Mohrman

93

Festival of Balloons

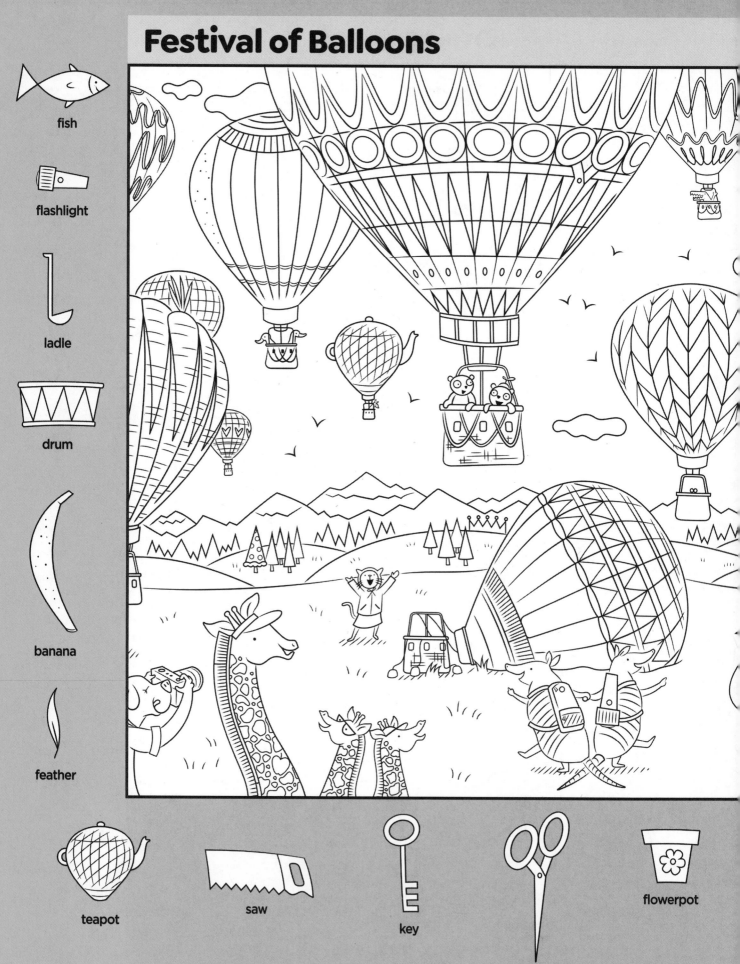

fish

flashlight

ladle

drum

banana

feather

teapot

saw

key

scissors

flowerpot

slice of pizza

toothbrush

mushroom

purse

rolling pin

carrot

toothpaste

peanut

crown

belt

apple

ladder

Art by Christine Schneider

Scuba Cats

butterfly

banana

heart

mushroom

pennant

carrot

spool of thread

butter knife

pliers

crayon

toothbrush

worm

tube of toothpaste

comb

sandal

headphones

egg

horseshoe

Art by Rocky Fuller

96

Swingin' on Rings

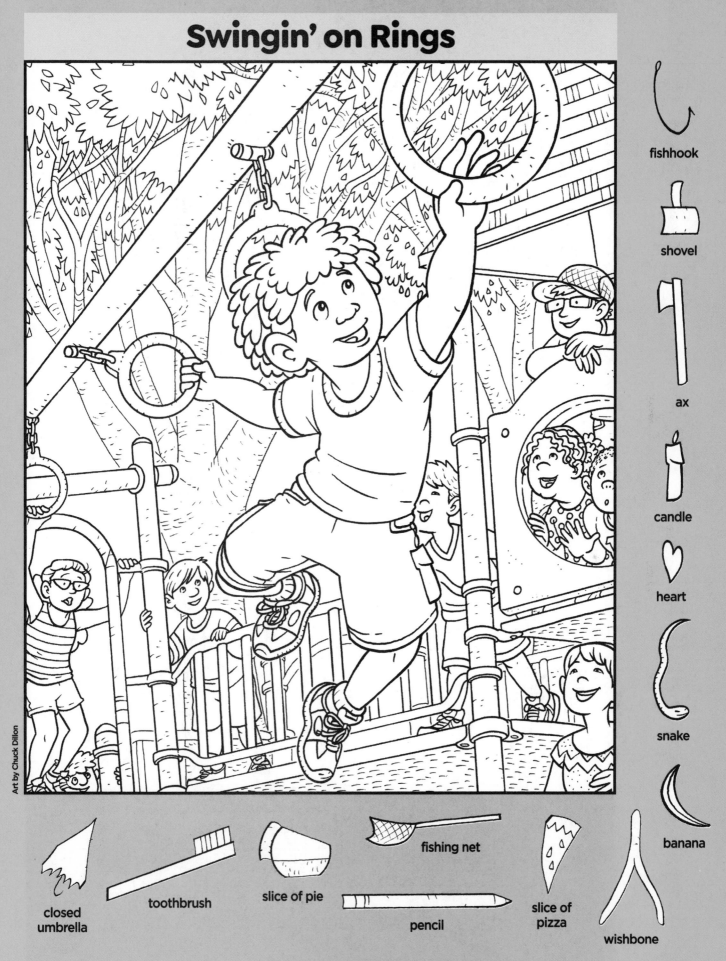

Art by Chuck Dillon

fishhook

shovel

ax

candle

heart

snake

banana

closed
umbrella

toothbrush

slice of pie

fishing net

pencil

slice of
pizza

wishbone

Sprints

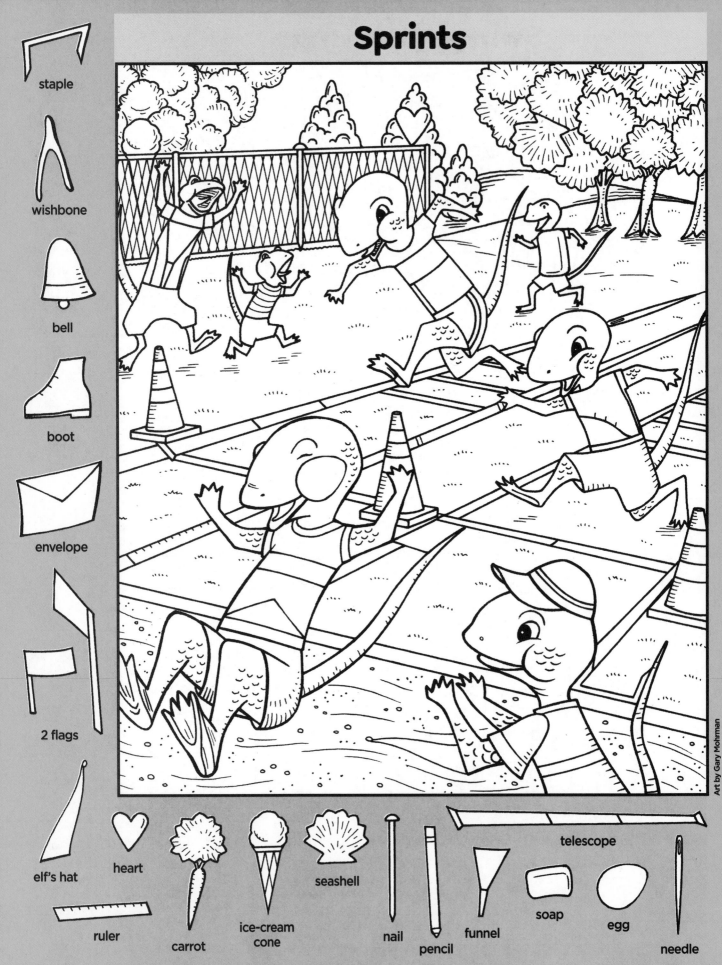

staple

wishbone

bell

boot

envelope

2 flags

elf's hat

heart

ruler

carrot

ice-cream cone

seashell

nail

pencil

funnel

soap

telescope

egg

needle

Art by Gary Mohrman

Rappelling

needle

handbell

elf's hat

spoon

mug

tack

tube of
toothpaste

pennant

ice-cream
cone

nail

safety
pin

slipper

Art by R. Michael Palan

99

Monster Truck Rally

comb

crescent moon

umbrella

eyeglasses

candy corn

mug

sailboat

snow cone

ring

tack

wedge of lemon

traffic light

safety pin

bowl

ladle

leaf

100

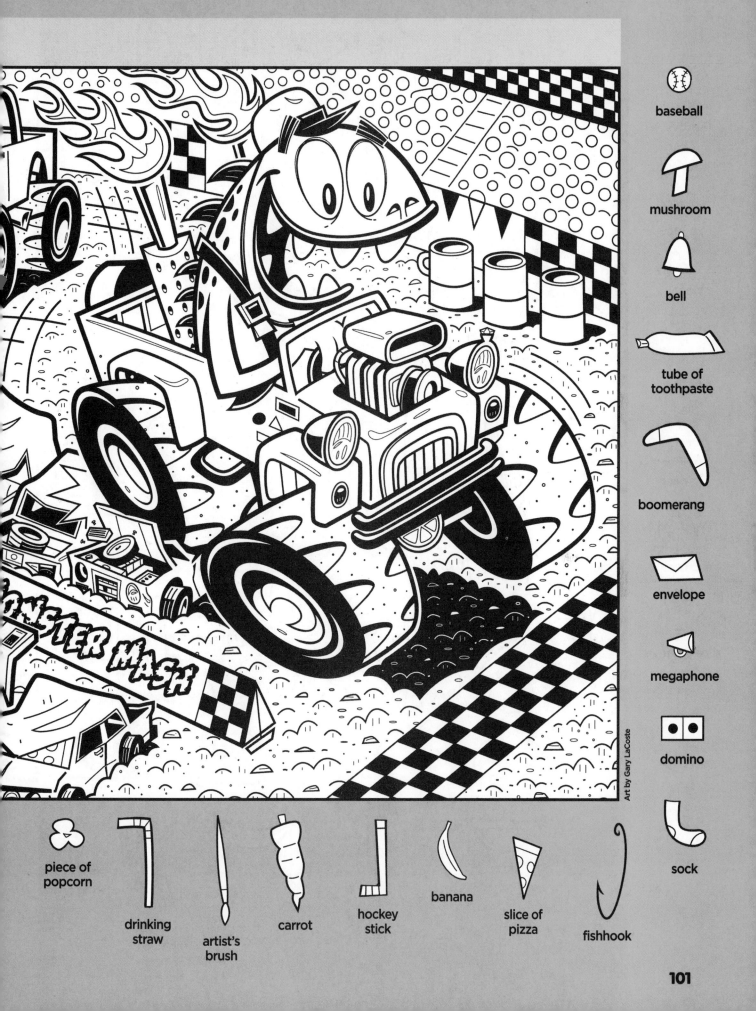

baseball

mushroom

bell

tube of
toothpaste

boomerang

envelope

megaphone

domino

sock

piece of
popcorn

drinking
straw

artist's
brush

carrot

hockey
stick

banana

slice of
pizza

fishhook

Art by Gary LaCoste

101

The Ice Wall

bowling ball

broccoli

paper clip

can

needle

ruler

crown

slice of bread

sock

snake

bowl

ring

domino

bat

ladder

canoe

envelope

fishhook

watering can

Art by Pat Lewis

Paddle Surfers

ghost

slice of cake

ruler

baseball bat

grapes

fishhook

artist's brush

elf's hat

feather

whale

sea star

vase

magician's wand

ladder

balloon

boot

open book

glove

rabbit

drumstick

Art by Gary Mohrman

103

What a Catch!

muffin

banana

candle

tack

slice of pie

glove

artist's brush

chicken

candy corn

lamp

pen

carrot

mitten

bell

slice of pizza

envelope

pencil

toothbrush

butter knife

Art by Chuck Dillon

Backyard Zippers

flag

spool of thread

wishbone

crescent moon

drinking glass

heart

magnet

ice-cream cone

crayon

bar of soap

slice of cake

wedge of cheese

sock

bowl

flashlight

seashell

slice of pie

Art by Gary Mohrman

105

Lunar Landscape

broom

game
piece

fork

book

magnet

peanut

crayon

adhesive
bandage

toothbrush

high-heeled
shoe

mitten

lollipop

Art by Patrick Girouard

Iditarod Trail Adventure

Art by Tamara Petrosino

adhesive
bandage

baseball
glove

slice of pie

caterpillar

ruler

2 pennants

sailboat

lightning bolt

snake

iron

paintbrush

envelope

banana

butter knife

108

Monkeying Around

mushroom

sock

zipper

candle

olive

pennant

peanut

umbrella

sailboat

shoe

fishhook

heart

baseball cap

glove

strawberry

paper clip

scissors

Art by Deborah Johnson

Ski School

crown

fish

toothbrush

flag

pencil

rabbit

crayon

candy corn

paintbrush

wedge of lemon

110

birthday cake

bell

can

dog bone

yo-yo

drinking straw

dolphin

envelope

boomerang

letter *H*

Art by Dana Regan

111

Demolition Derby Night!

ice-cream bar

teacup

leaf

bird

sock

crescent moon

harmonica

nail

lollipop

domino

key

waffle

pennant

telescope

adhesive bandage

spoon

Art by Brian Michael Weaver

112

Leaps and Bounds

book

banana

boomerang

cupcake

comb

fishhook

party hat

umbrella

broccoli

heart

pencil

toothbrush

domino

saucepan

slice of cake

canoe

musical note

snake

fish

Art by Pat Lewis

Wild Water

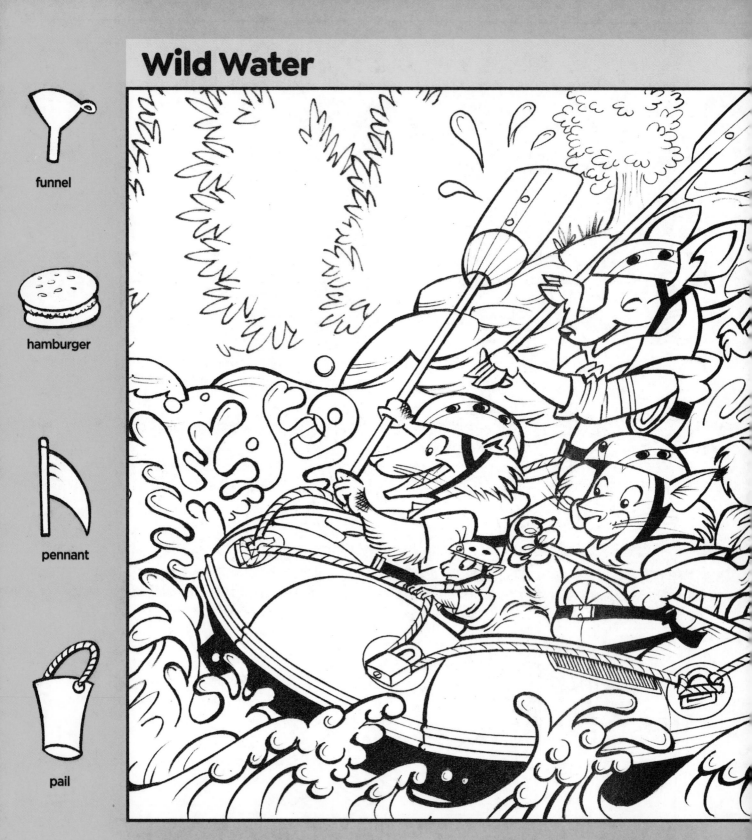

funnel

hamburger

pennant

pail

ladybug

loaf of bread

bow

candy cane

fan

lock

wedge of orange

tape dispenser

mug

shoe

screwdriver

comb

Art by Rocky Fuller

Unicycle Day

bell

lollipop

candle

sailboat

banana

slice of pizza

ruler

crown

golf club

toothbrush

tube of toothpaste

mug

heart

bowl

crescent moon

mushroom

pennant

fishhook

hockey stick

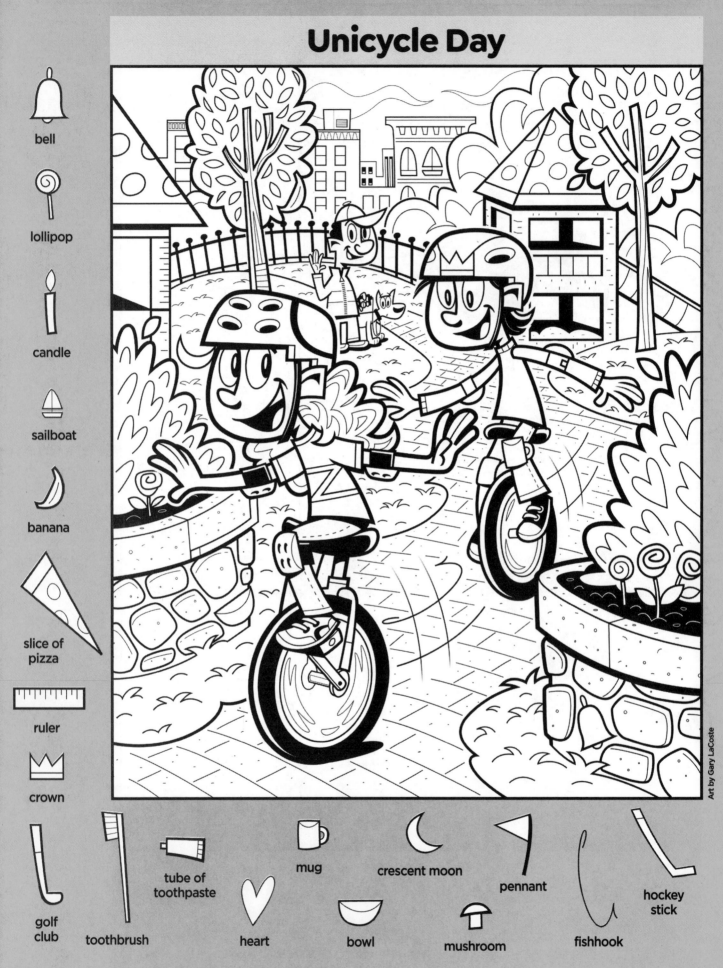

Art by Gary LaCoste

116

Race to the Bottom

artist's brush

lollipop

pennant

carrot

bell

mitten

funnel

crown

hammer

cane

fishhook

needle

mushroom

ring

sandwich

toothbrush

mug

crescent moon

tack

heart

drinking straw

bird

Art by R. Michael Palan

117

Mountain Bikes

boomerang

golf club

crescent moon

drinking glass

tack

ladle

butter knife

candle

sock

banana

doughnut

raindrop

feather

slice of pie

seashell

lettuce

crown

needle

Art by Gary Mohrman

Skippy the Pilot

banana

shuttlecock

fork

tack

high-heeled shoe

sock

toy top

carrot

boot

table-tennis paddle

ice-cream cone

horn

eyeglasses

doughnut

crescent moon

Art by George Wildman

Roller Moose

present

screwdriver

baby's bottle

chili pepper

saltshaker

fork

spoon

turtle

mallet

mitten

funnel

drinking
glass

doughnut

hoe

Art by Iryna Bodnaruk

121

Monkey Climbers

bird

fish

spatula

chili pepper

slice of cake

teacup

wishbone

pennant

needle

lollipop

fried egg

crescent moon

wedge of orange

pine tree

seashell

mushroom

ice-cream cone

slice of pizza

adhesive bandage

sea star

Art by Gary Mohrman

Surf's Up!

candy cane

slice of pizza

flashlight

tack

ladder

envelope

teacup

bat

spatula

mallet

spoon

paper airplane

fried egg

Art by Jackie Stafford

Stalagmites and Stalactites

fork

bell

artist's brush

key

fish

spoon

mitten

carrot

124

pennant

rocket ship

comb

shoe

hat

lollipop

wishbone

sock

Art by Mike DeSantis

125

Down We Go!

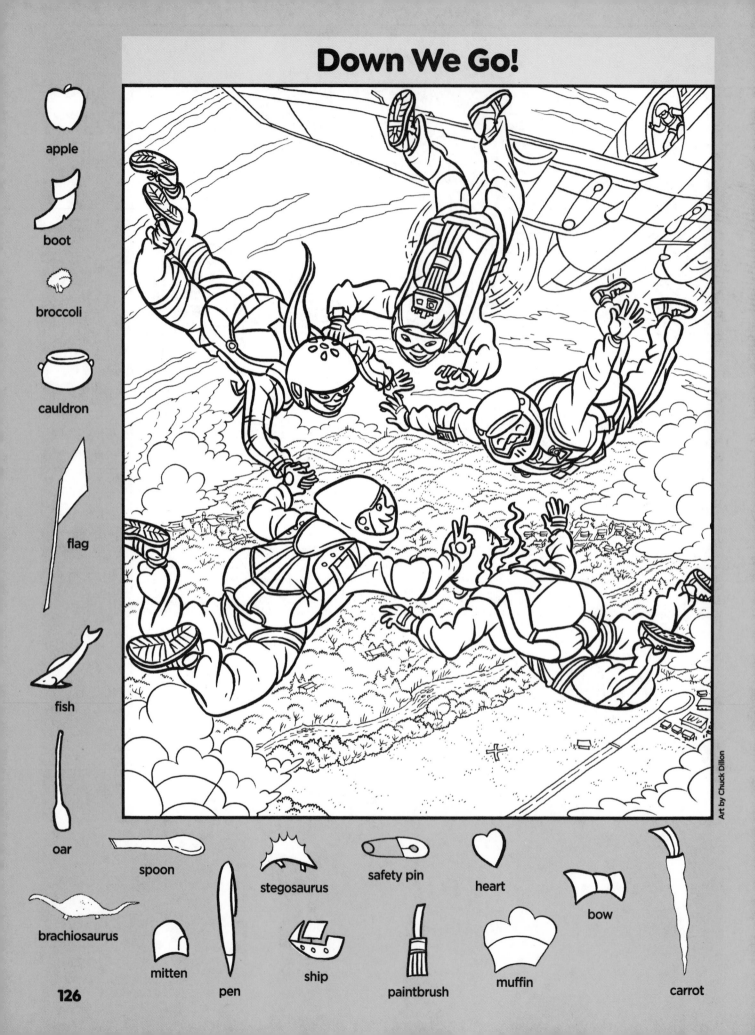

apple

boot

broccoli

cauldron

flag

fish

oar

brachiosaurus

spoon

stegosaurus

safety pin

heart

bow

mitten

pen

ship

paintbrush

muffin

carrot

Art by Chuck Dillon

126

Go-Kart Race

crescent moon

bell

pencil

nail

ring

spoon

drumstick

mallet

banana

slice of pizza

toothbrush

horseshoe

musical note

needle

ice-cream cone

screwdriver

Art by R. Michael Palan

127

Wheel Fun

spoon

banana

umbrella

wedge of lemon

candy cane

baby's bottle

flashlight

slice of pizza

kite

artist's brush

envelope

heart

toothbrush

hat

ice-cream cone

paintbrush

hoe

Art by Jennifer Harney

Answers

▼ Pages 4–5

▼ Page 6

▼ Page 7

▼ Page 8

▼ Page 9

▼ Page 10

▼ Page 11

▼ Page 12

Answers

▼Page 13

▼Pages 14–15

▼Page 16

▼Page 17

▼Page 18

▼Page 19

▼Page 20

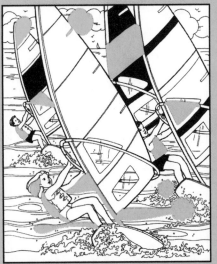

▼Page 21

Answers

▼Pages 22-23

▼Page 24

▼Page 25

▼Pages 26-27

▼Page 28

▼Page 29

▼Page 30

Answers

▼Page 31

▼Page 32

▼Page 33

▼Pages 34–35

▼Page 36

▼Page 37

▼Page 38

▼Page 39

Answers

▼Pages 40–41

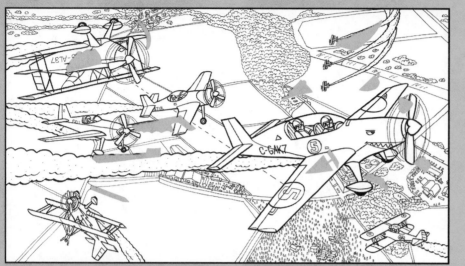

▼Page 42

▼Page 43

▼Pages 44–45

▼Page 46

▼Page 47

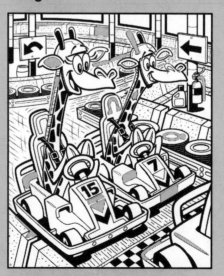

▼Page 48

▼Page 49

▼Pages 50–51

▼Page 52

▼Page 53

▼Pages 54–55

▼Page 56

Answers

▼ Page 57

▼ Page 58

▼ Page 59

▼ Pages 60–61

▼ Page 62

▼ Page 63

▼ Page 64

▼ Page 65

Answers

▼Page 66

▼Page 67

▼Page 68

▼Page 69

▼Pages 70–71

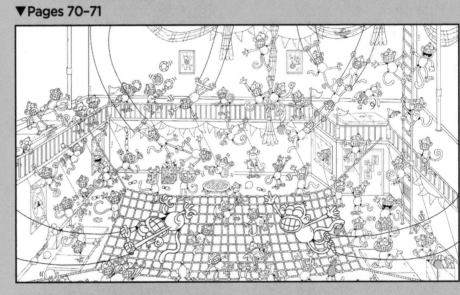

▼Page 72

▼Page 73

▼Page 74

Answers

▼Page 75

▼Pages 76–77

▼Page 78

▼Page 79

▼Page 80

▼Page 81

▼Pages 82–83

Answers

▼Page 84

▼Page 85

▼Page 86

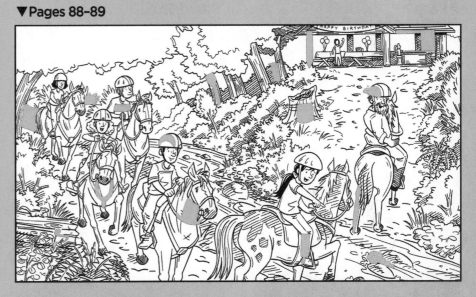

▼Page 87

▼Pages 88–89

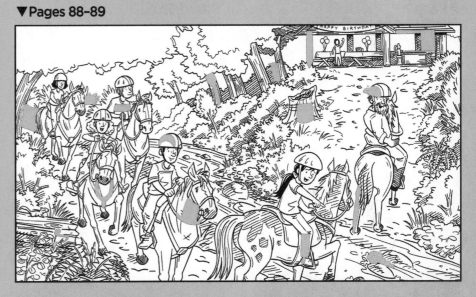

▼Page 90

▼Page 91

▼Page 92

Answers

▼**Page 93**

▼**Pages 94–95**

▼**Page 96**

▼**Page 97**

▼**Page 98**

▼**Page 99**

▼**Pages 100–101**

Answers

▼Page 102

▼Page 103

▼Page 104

▼Page 105

▼Pages 106–107

▼Page 108

▼Page 109

Answers

▼ Pages 110–111

▼ Page 112

▼ Page 113

▼ Pages 114–115

▼ Page 116

▼ Page 117

▼ Page 118

Answers

▼Page 119

▼Pages 120–121

▼Page 122

▼Page 123

▼Pages 124–125

▼Page 126

Answers

▼Page 127

▼Pages 128–129

For information about permission to reprint
selections from this book, please contact
permissions@highlights.com.

Published by Highlights Press
815 Church Street, Honesdale, Pennsylvania 18431
ISBN: 978-1-64472-864-2
Manufactured in Robbinsville, NJ, USA
Mfg. 07/2023
First edition
Visit our website at Highlights.com.
10 9 8 7 6 5 4 3 2